# COSTA RICA

N

"TRAVEL MAKES ONE MODEST. YOU SEE WHAT A TINY PLACE YOU OCCUPY IN THE WORLD." – GUSTAVE FLAUBERT

*This book was authored and illustrated by Christy Connell (Cricky). After spending two years traveling around North, Central, and South America, Cricky was inspired to merge her love of travel with her love of art, and a series of coloring books was born. Please enjoy Costa Rican Creatures: A Traveler's Coloring Book!!!

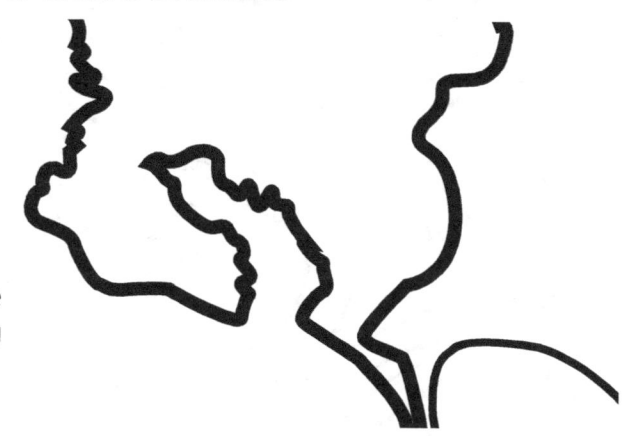

# one ocelot

## un ocelote [OON oh-say-LOH-tay]

Unlike most cats, ocelots are strong swimmers.

# two toucans
# dos tucánes

[DOHS too-CAHN'-es]

Toucans use their large beaks to reach fruit on branches too small to support their weight.

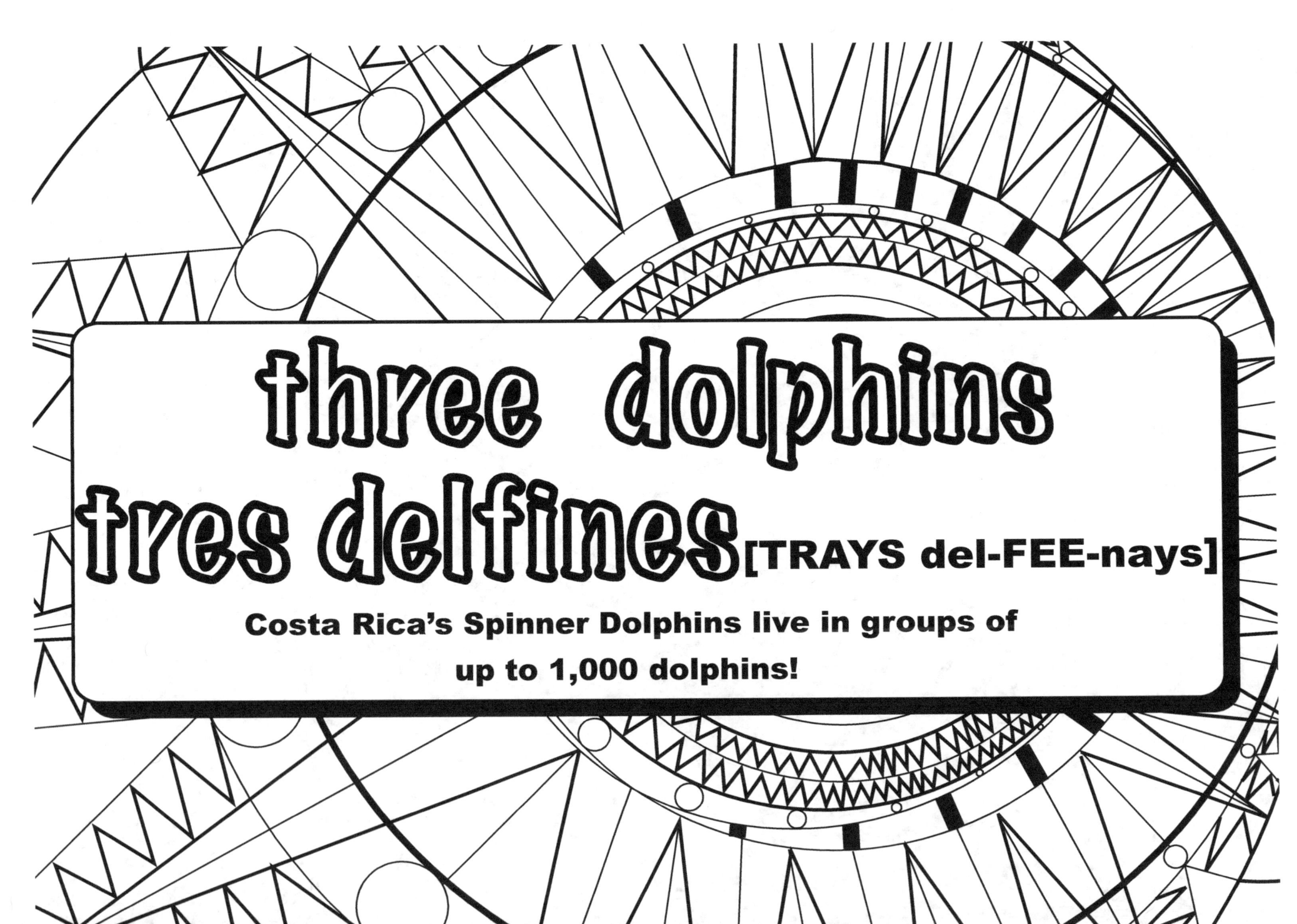

# three dolphins
# tres delfines [TRAYS del-FEE-nays]

**Costa Rica's Spinner Dolphins live in groups of up to 1,000 dolphins!**

# four sloths
# cuatro perezosos

**[coo-AH-tro pay-ray-SOH-sos]**

**Sloths move so slowly that algae, cockroaches, and beetles often live in their fur.**

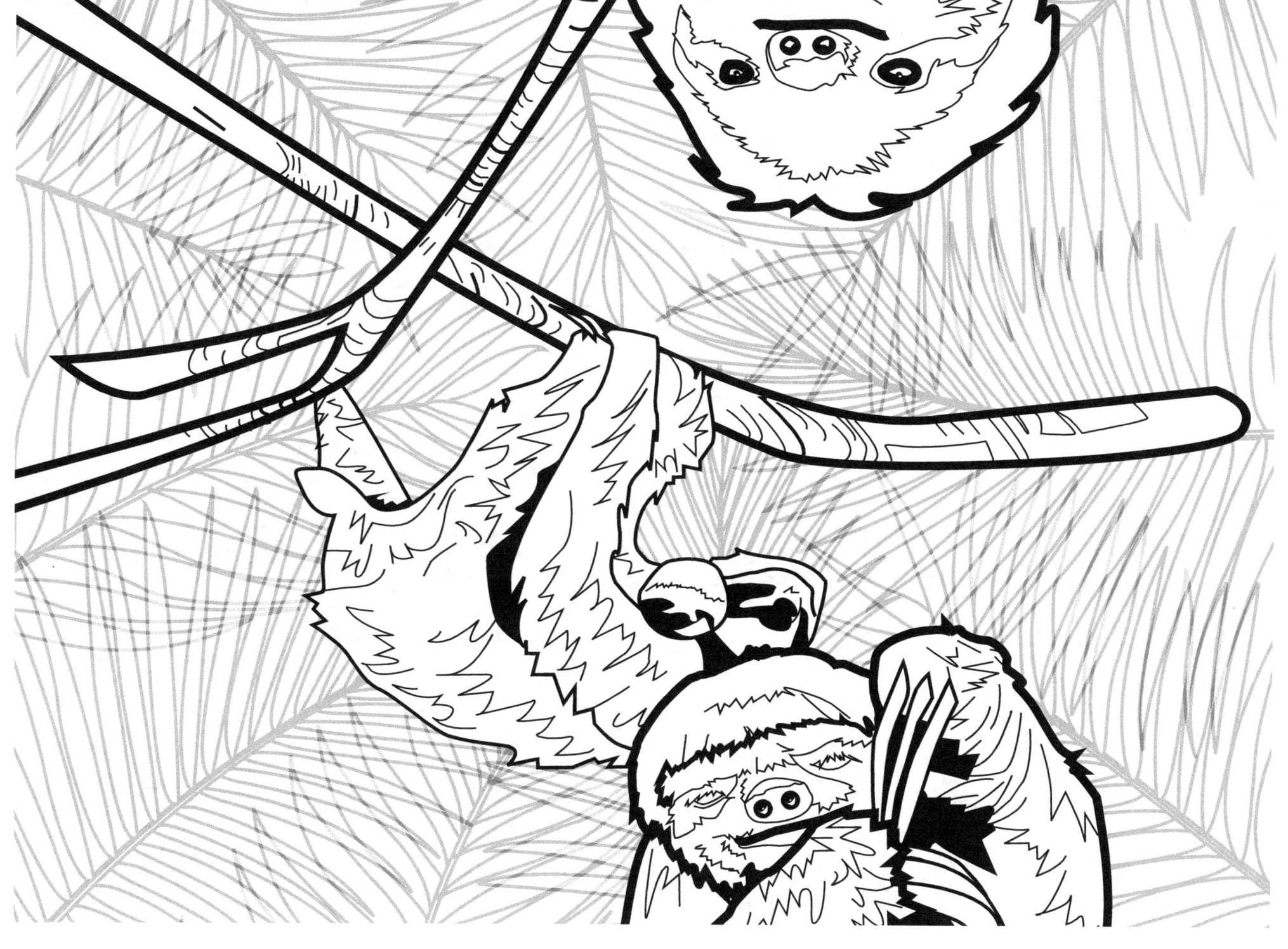

# five howler monkeys
## cinco congos

[SEEN-coh COHN-gohs]

Howler monkeys make loud vocal sounds that can be heard up to three miles away in the jungle.

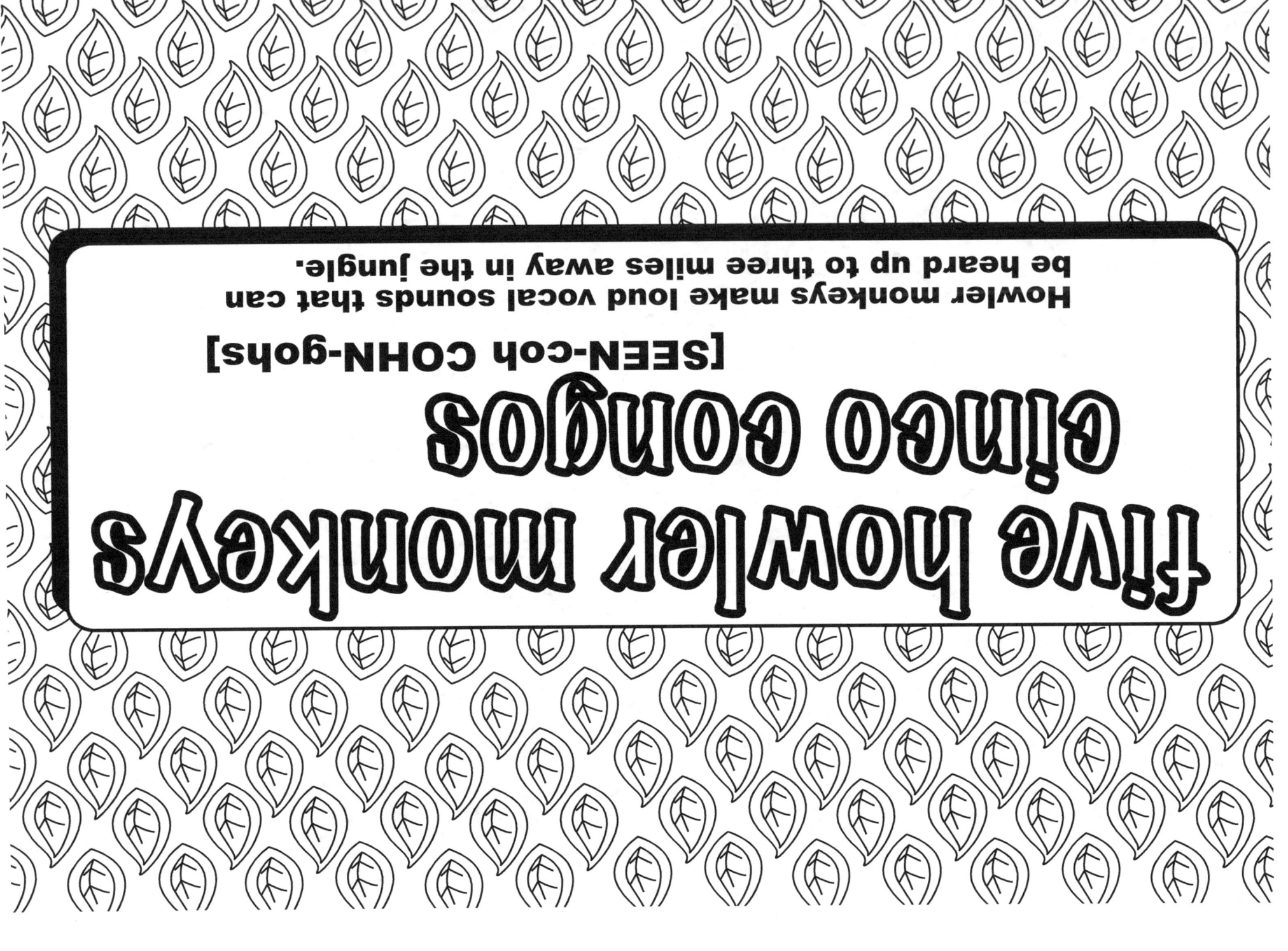

# 6 basilisks

## seis basiliscos

[SAY-s bah-see-LEES-kohs]

Basilisks can run on the water's surface to escape predators.

# seven crocodiles
# siete cocodrilos

[see-AY-tay COH-coh-DREE-lohs]

**Costa Rica's crocodiles can grow up to 20 feet (6.1 meters) long!**

# eight bats
## ocho murciélagos

**[OH-choh moo-er-see-AY-la-GOHS]**

**Vampire bats feed by biting their animal prey and licking the blood from the cut they made!**

# nine scorpions
# nueve escorpiones

[noo-AY-vay eh-SCOR-pee-OH-nays]

The sting of Costa Rica's scorpions is no worse than a bee sting.

# ten moths
# diez polillas

[dee-YAYS poh-LEE-yahs]

The harmless Wasp Moth's coloring mimics a wasp, which most predators are happy to avoid.

# tamandua

## tamanduá

**[tah-MAHN'-doo-AH]**

**Tamanduas are small anteaters that release a skunklike scent to ward off predators like jaguars and harpy eagles.**